BASICS OF BREATHING

Poetry by

Heini Talip

Printed in the United States of America

First Printing, 2020

ISBN 978-1-949321-16-6

All writings within this book belong to the author.

Cover Art & Design by: Heini Talip

A.B.Baird Publishing
66548 Highway 203
La Grande OR, 97850
USA

www.abbairdpublishing.com

To my husband.
I am not whole without you. Or a poet.

To all those who help animals.
Never give up.

HUNGRY

I exist
in the scrutiny of my saliva,
asking
always just
asking

begging

for answers,
for sustenance.

Printed

This agony
is shapeless,
a feverish fluid
distributed
in the silence of my blood,
at times coated
on the roof of my mouth,
hidden
for the palm reader
to decipher,
pain printed on me.

WRONG SHINE

In the marble shine of stars,
we
the dusty leftovers
with our shiny foreheads
think we can shimmer too.

Fine Print

Life checks the box
with fine ink pen,
writes us
unintelligibly.

All of us spend eternity
underlining,
highlighting, smudging
what was printed.

PAST LIVES

Past lives I think I have had:

Fingers entangled on a chain-link fence.

Shooting star that didn't ignite falling.

A flower with a black eye.

INSIDE

Yes, yes.

Hide it all
wherever you have room.

Try that throbbing thing
ruining your chest, or
the roots of your toothache,
the folds of your flesh
heck,
put it all
inside those wells
that never hold their water.

GHOST

Forever will forget you.
And never needs a note
with your name.

DOT

A dot.

An ink drop
on the cursive of cosmos.
A dab
of human humidity
against a desert of dark.

That's all.
Ever.

OUTLINES

Mostly I am
just
fingertips tracing
lines I wish I didn't have.

DEAF

The wing strokes of a butterfly.
The formation of a sigh.
Marching of clouds.

Do they make a sound?

SPILL

It was all
just infected illumination,
fake smiles
on cheekbones of cosmos
chemistry in a cocktail
and then
us
with our morals and molars
soft and blunt
no match for
this world and
the carnivore clouds and
the honest lines of arrows,
stars spilled
and the bleach of our being
trying to clean up the crime scene.

SALTY SOUL

I've become so good at it
tears approach me now
volunteering to be cried through me.

CROSSROADS

Who can blame
this poor blood of mine
pausing at the crossroads of veins
trying to decide whether to go,
or not.

ARTISTIC AGONY

Pain is a painter
and I am
the endless supply of canvases.
Pose for me,
it says,
piercing me
with those watercolor forks.
And the artist's signature
is always scribbled down my cheek.

FRAGILE

Don't chisel
for a sample of my soul.
I am
geography
of glass.

LAYERS

This universe of mine
peels
in layers of landscapes
I will never see:

Atomic alignments,
skin deep settlements of flesh and bone,
human haze
(here place me)
mud and clay of the earth,
and pottery of the living,
then
cloudy stairwells
and the weaving of planetary plush,
all the abyss above
realms and rust of eternity
tinted in ink that spilled
all over this fabric of
space and time.

INGREDIENT

Am I allowed to envy my breath
for becoming an ingredient of sky?

BRICK

I'm just an abyss
and the soul they tossed me
a brick
going straight to the bottom.

CAUTIOUSLY

Can it be
happiness
when you catch the arm of the clock move?
When a sunset makes you smile?
When a hand lands on a chest, a flight departs?
When rain fights umbrellas? And beneath I smile?

DEHYDRATED

Are my stinging eyes
just a compliment for cosmos?
Are all these tears just watering the pain,
something for the dehydrated darkness to
call rain?

WATERS OF WANTING

I am
moisture on madness,
waters of wanting,
wet
in the teardrop shape
of
me.

VIOLINS

We are
meat and marrows
playing
the violin music of rust.

Turn it Around

Couldn't eternity have neat edges?
Couldn't dandelion dust blow me apart?
Couldn't clouds wear the sky?
A circle speak in straight lines?
A human exhale and not be a sigh?

Lavender Lighthouses

Tell me about
the longing
in the lavender of bruises,
the spin
of blind lighthouses,
tell me
why this life
blends
these opposite dyes?

REALITY/*REALITY*

I'm okay. I'm okay.
I tell myself
smiling over the sink, over the slumped toothbrush,
the used up bar of soap,
over the moisturizing cream that promised
rejuvenation.
I'm okay.
But why do I always swallow when I say that?

DARKEST DEEP

I imagine
this universe
just stands there
with a dripping paint brush
wondering
if it chose the right shade.

SOUL, THE ASTRONAUT

Venture past the atmosphere of animation,
darkness
and decimal points of me,
find a spot
(there is plenty!)
and float free.

NOTE TO UNIVERSE

Our foreheads
are the worst spots
to stick post-it notes.

WIREHANGER

In the closet of darkness,

me

a
wilted
wirehanger
soul.

ON/OFF

Every star
is a flickering lightbulb
about to go out.

Every soul
is a light switch
dusted for fingerprints.

Every abyss
has a flashlight
for its own murkiness.

FLOAT

I adore
the clumsiness of a paper airplane, the
panic of a hummingbird, dandelions
and their corpses in the wind, and
a lone feather falling, dragging its feet, watching
a leaf of fall
coming down.

I love things that can float,
even if just for a while.

BRUISED

Hit by the elbow of eternity.

Chewed by the teeth of stars.

How does one not get hurt here?

Rainbow

We rummaged all the raindrops
and it was barely there
the rainbow
we wanted.

WAYS I WISH TO DIE:

Cursive curses or
soft-spoken bullets,
fever of daydreaming or
pillow fights of poison.

LIFE

I am
bleeding profusely
from the papercut I got
turning a page
on a book that said:
Life:
Important Instructions
Read me.

Door Knob

If Universe was a room,
it would have cold tile floors,
a door knob that doesn't work
and a draft.

Soul

Is a soul a slope or a flat surface?
I think some atoms are complaining.

THIS

This reached out hand
this
bouquet of nerve endings
this
weight of soul and separation
is me.
This
pain and pebble
this blinking blindness
it will always be me.

STORY I WRITE

I need
blank pages,
paperclips of pain,
ink in
blackest black
sharpener (for self defense)
red pen for the typos,
capital letters for the screams
and in the end
an eraser.

MEANINGLESS

No, you don't see me.
But how could you?
I exist
like the blush of a brick wall.
I am that line
your pen drew
to test the ink.

BEGGAR

Oh, I believe.

I worship
in the cathedral
of my cupped hands.

BACKSEAT

Isn't it life
when we are sleeping on this steel soil
dreaming of the plush pillows of stars?
Isn't it
us sitting in the backseat of existence
asking:
Are we there yet?
Are we there yet?
Are we there yet?

ART

I am
panic in a picture frame.
I am
an ink test
for stressed out stars,
a portrait
of what not to become
(atoms 101).

SHORE OF MY FEARS

See?

A fallen leaf
floating across a puddle.

Nothing to it.
Easy peasy.

It can be done,
I try to tell my soul,
that shivering thing
sitting on the shore of my fears.

BREAK ME

I just need

something
   anything

to scatter these atoms
like I was pool balls
arranged in an abyss.

DUSTY

We're all stardust.

Blah, blah, blah.

And this universe has got to be asthmatic.

DEEP END OF THE POOL

We need a top
and a bottom.

Roof.
Walls. Hardwood floors.
Outlines and borders.
Crust and coating.
Arrows to point things.

We need a sign at the deep end of the pool:
No diving!

But still we drown there.

STING

This won't hurt a bit.

Says the cosmos
inking my injuries,
all while
pressing the pillow of pitch black
on my snow white soul.

CONGRATULATIONS

That metal taste in your mouth
could be
the trophy you wanted
for being alive.

PLAN

Was it a mistake
to write this night with such ink?
And these cracks of our mouths?
This darkness of our drool?
These daggers of our declarations of love,
they were also the plan?

PISS

Stars piss.
Darkness flushes the toilet.
And I exist in that sad abyss.

BUBBLE

I am inside
the thought bubble of this universe
Right?

Right?

FOOLISH

I'm trying.
I'm flapping my wings on this breath of space.
It's freaking freezing.
Like ice cold.
And I don't really have wings.
I'm just moving my arms.

      Foolish.
         I know.

HOW CRUEL

How do we know eternity doesn't exist
expecting a moment of impact?

BLUE IS A BREATHING COLOR

Sadness sits
in the heaven of holding my breath.
Despair dilutes into tear-shaped bricks.
Shade of a bruise cools my skin.

Blue is my becoming.
Blue is a breathing color.

FOG

A soul
is not a fiber, a
marble, a
glowing light.

A soul is
a fog of flesh, a
drizzle, a
weather of wanting to be alive.

BLINK

I wish
space would blink.

I mean
imagine:

Death by eyelids.
Demise by divine eye boogers.
Slaughter by a staring contest.

That's the way to go.

MANICURES

I wonder
if the universe feels pain
from all these nails
clawing from within?

PADDED

Do dreams have soft curves
so when they shatter
they won't cut us?

This Shade

Whatever color moonlight is.
Dip me in that.
Anything but
this shade of soul.

QUESTIONS I HAVE

Are my atoms ever tired of always being dressed as
me?
(I'm not that fashionable)
Are nasal-sounding nightmares just ill, or defective?
(my dreams must be allergic to me)
Do stars give speeches to space we never get to hear?
(I want front row seats!)

POP!

Barbwire decorated hearts
in a ballooning universe.

Who's gonna be the one to pop it?

COLOR OF FAREWELL

Goodbyes.
See ya laters.
Hands slipping from hands.
The blush of endings
smudges us all
on the pale coloring books
we are.

TABLECLOTH

Fabric of time and space:
is it silk
or some cheap polyester?

Or are we all just dying on a tablecloth
on divine dinner time?

BE KIND

Stepping over an ant is compassion.

Universe grinding us to powder
can be compassion too.

Rebellion

It's all just another way
we push against this cosmos. Rebel.

These breaths we take. Exhale.
These eyes shot upward. Staring.
These virgin sheets of paper we crumble up. Toss.
These ill-postured backs. Turned.

We rebel.
Sick with our stardust.

TIRED

I'm tired.
I exist
exhausted
in the yellow of my yawns,
all my dreams
running down the legs of life.

CRACKS

In the end
I just wish
for whiteness of wells
light
something
like the glow of television
sparks
sparingly
but often
and cracks
in the luster of dark
so I know
not to fall.

BEING

I'm a landscape,
a being,
a bridge of collarbones,
mountain peaks of knuckles,
a scenery sinned
from conception to conclusion.

LUNGS

Hold your breath. Dive.
Drown,
lungs like over-packed suitcases.

Or just die slowly
of the second-hand smoke of space.

Either way,
you're suffocating.

LANGUAGE I UNDERSTAND

Speak to me in:
the bell tolls of tight spaces
grin of color grey
long vowels of whales
hurried slurps of the sea.
Speak to me
like this
and I will listen.

I TRY

I try to travel
this tranquility of torment
with you.
I try
with bloody knees
and a bruised heart.
I try
with the determination of dust
pale before the puckered lips of god.

LISTEN

All I get is
squeaky shopping carts and
wailing babies and
honking and
sirens and
alarm clocks and
the sound of me ripping toilet paper.

What it sounds like
when this universe chafes on another
I'll never know.

ORGANS OF DAYDREAMS

Aren't I
just accidental anatomy surveying a soul?
Aren't I
just organs of daydreams,
a frame of bones
with the factory photo still inside?

NATURAL STATE OF STARS

Serrated
coiled
confused
is
the natural state of stars
(like mine)
both just
tired of
twinkle twinkle.

SCABS

Bleeding
is this universe breathing.
We're just the scabs it loves to pick on.

TALE

I'm a blinking cursor.
A line on an empty screen.
Waiting.
Waiting for the typing.
Words.
Any words.
What font am I?
Do I have typos?
Will my tale
please the punctuation mark?

WHAT RAIN WANTS

Cement of clouds
undressed umbrellas
me
soaked to my skeleton
hanging my heart on the clothesline to dry.

AUTHOR

If you could place an ear on my soul
and listen
from the hum
of heartbeat and flesh
you could make out
the flutter of the pages caught in the wind
like I'm always looking for my chapter,
my page,
my place.

And my author.

STEP ON THE SCALE

Souls are skinny things.
I don't weigh
here
now
in this shaving of space
enough to
give an atom an itch.

DISCOMFORT

Adorable pain:
Hit your leg on the table and the bruise is the shape of
a heart. Aww.

Painful adoring:
Look at the night sky
and wonder what it would feel like to stick your head
into the cold void of space?

ART OF PULSE

Would it be any different
if our hearts spoke in another way?
Not in sharp peaks,
flatlines
or serpentine strokes.
What if we drew our pulses
in knots or even
spirals?
What if we
vibrated
in the shape of pretty bows?
Would it make any difference?

GOOD BOY

I swear
universe has us for pets.
We come here already leashed
in our umbilical cords.

MASCARA

Sure,
I cried my mascara
all over my cheeks.
So what?
Everyday here ends
with sun smearing
on the lash line of night.

FLESH

This world
sprouts teeth and blossoms bullets.
Beware
soft pink thing, you
flavor of clenched fists.
Anything of flesh
is either naked,
bandaged
or hanging upside down.

TAKE ME TO THE BEACH

Is there
an ocean in an atom
somewhere in me?
Do the waves
tutor my saliva?
Does the monsoon
mimic my breath?
What hum
do the seashells
whisper there?

LIFE SUPPORT

Be real quiet
and you'll hear the beep
of a life support machine
whistling in my nostrils.
Me breathing at all
is CPR for the soul.

TOWEL

Who has the towel
for the nudity of my dreams?

HUMAN DILEMMAS

Aren't we
just milky mouths
in decorated darkness?
Dried up ink pens
trying to salivate on paper?
Choices of cells
to divide or die?

DRUNK

We couldn't walk a straight line if we wanted to.
Our atoms spin
tipsy on our twilight.
And I'm pretty sure
this universe is
far from being sober.

PILLOW

Sometimes
the only thing that reminds you you're still alive is a
cool spot on the pillow
you've been laying on
hammering your good dreams
inside the walls your sad skull.

DEFINITION OF DIMPLES

I imagine if stars wrote the manual
on human existence,
the definition of dimples would be:

Even in joy
these creatures crack.
Strange things.

I agree.

ASPIRIN

I hurt.
You hurt.
The walls of this house hurt.
Faucets scream bloody murder
and our hairs in the drain haunt us
accusing our scalps of murder.
Fuck.
Everything aches.
Even heartbreak has a headache.
Life should be
a spokesperson for aspirin.

HEART-SHAPED

Sadness
likes me
with the crust cut off.
Just the soft parts,
defenseless
preferably pressed into a heart-shaped cookie cutter.
So the world can go aww.

Breaking Heaven

Sky will fall
    one day
and it will be done
by the fury of a snowflake,
fist of a cloud
and the sledgehammer of a raindrop.

BOOKMARK

You folded the corner, right?
Bookmarked it,
didn't you?
That part you liked,
that little chapter of my soul,
that verse
of my universe,
that starry scroll
unrolled in darkness.
You didn't forget,
did you?
I am still
the best damn poetry
vibrating on your nerves?

HOUSEKEEPING

In the end
(I hope)
this universe will bust out the duster
and the vacuum,
put some drain cleaner down the pipes,
perhaps even
polish the silver.

For the new quests.

NAIL BITER

How to stop your soul from biting its nails.
I haven't found a YouTube tutorial for that one yet.

ANXIETY

Rip off
pages of a child's coloring book
and show them to my soul.

There you are
silly
stardust with anxiety.

LINT OF LIGHT

All those sunsets
slipped across our eyeballs,
do they polish us
or scrape us
for lint of light?

BASICS OF BREATHING

Inhale
exhale
oil this oxygen,
bless it
for the light at the end of the tunnel,
sigh
like stardust
stuck in a jar.
Repeat.

POLLUTION

I wish
the world behind my dirty windows
was a pollution of petals,
not this
mouldy darkness
calling itself cosmic.

SPIT

This beautiful dark
grins a stellar smile

and the growl

   g r o w l

of its hunger
drips down the celestial chin
and we

   w e

are just faint lines
in the silhouette of its spit.

Janitor

This place
has no wet floor signs,
no
towels
for the spilled stars,
no
broom
for the dandruff of darkness,
no
janitor
to bring the bucket
when the ceiling of our cell
begins to leak.

LIFEBOAT

our lips
the broken dams

from first breath
we contaminate

first words
we salivate
and soon
we need a lifeboat.

FOR THE MOUSE THAT DIED IN THE GLUE TRAP

This world is an adhesive for innocence.
It traps us, breaks our breaths
and suffocates our spines.

I'm sorry,
I'm trying to free myself too.

SHOVEL

I am a buried being
padded inside my flesh
born with the costume of a coffin.
I am a grain of dust
shoveled
somewhat neatly
into a pile of human.

BALLOONS

There is no perfect seam in a soul.
Those loose strings are how
this gravity
tugs me to this cosmic clay.
We're basically
balloons
in the slippery hands of space.

VISUALLY IMPAIRED

Is it blindness
or bliss
that bathes me
with this darkness
ruptured
behind my lids?
Is it sadness
or solace
that ripples
to the water's edge
of my vision?

PIGMENT

I was once
a sigh
translucent in tranquility.
I was once
air
collecting flesh around me
but now
I am tired,

I am so tired

and I have become
painful pigment,
matching my abyss.

WATER DAMAGE

They say we're mostly made of water.
We leak it.
We hold it.
Melt and freeze.
Overflow
every time
in the mildew of our meat.
So most of us are
just sick souls
complaining about water damage.

HURT

Body parts we hurt the most by being alive:

Our hearts on the spoon of space.
Knees, scraped by the soil of stars.
Our eyes, oh, our eyes.

Spring

Do the branches of my breath know spring?
The unfurling of the feverish foliage?
Do I know that this chest
is the destination
of oxygen's migration route?

(Do I know? I don't know.)

ALL BLED OUT (A LOVE STORY)

This is an ugly love story, all of us
with these flesh wounds.

We fall in love, not rise
the whole thing already an accident.

No one knew first aid, we just
bandaged it,
let it fester.

We'll be fine, we said.

And here are,
souls the shade of sepsis,
hearts scarred,
all bled out.

THESE STUPID HANDS

How many
atoms have we crushed,
how many
prayers pressed,
between these hands?
These stupid hands.

WINDOW WASHER IN THE RAIN

I am lost.
Like a
window washer in the rain,
my existence
tangles.

FLAW (?)

This chest of mine
has a
b r e a t h l e s s
interior
and a
w i n d y
exterior.
And I suspect
many of us
are made the same.

WHICH DARK?

Do I choose
the sabre-toothed shadows of this world, or
the bruised grace
of space above?
Maybe
the dark I was coated with, or
the oil
polishing my eyeballs, or
the pitch-black
mocking my night light, or
perhaps
the one swirling ink
in the decanter of my soul?
Which one
do I go with?

UNKNOTTED

Perhaps life is
the suffocating noose
and death
the unravelling one
tied loose?

MOUTHS

This universe
is a swiveling bar stool.
Sit down
and get dizzy.
Here we drink
spiked lullabies
and sing
drunken dreams.

BECOMING

I become dust and
romance becomes ruins and
sky becomes wallpaper in heaven and
rain will become
the bottom of a bucket
drowning a fly.

CORE

I began from a sphere,
from a confused conception,
sadness the solitary cell
that multiplied in me.

NOSTRILS

Breathe.
Breathe.
Breathe.
You are not those
nervous nostrils
dilating in darkness,
aching
for asphyxia.
Ink your story with fog
against this
starry ravine.
Just
b r e a t h e.

BATH WATER FOR BONES

The way stars sleep
I wish to sleep:
soaked, still, supreme.
Darkness, dear,
have you prepared
the bath water for my bones?

Fizz

Aren't we eternally
always   *always*   *always*
in the process of
breaking
dissolving
with every lowering of eyelids
sweetly sinking
like nectar
nosediving into this abyss
our stardust
fizzing into a froth of the forgotten.

WINDOW

Why can't I be
like a window

open, yet sealed
glossed over
draped with dreams, decorated
with pretty little flower pots
that never wilt.

Why am I just an opening,
this gash
windy with my own waning?

TERMINATION

It is from the rainwater of never
collected in our navels
that this universe sips
when thirsty for termination.

LET IT COOL

I fear
within my windpipe,
to exhale
too hard
or too little
perhaps
my attempt to make
the temperature of tomorrow
lukewarm
not to burn my soul,
but
too late for that
I think.

ME AND YOU

I want to listen to
the pencil sounds of stars
wondering
how they sketch me
and you
on the same sheet of space.

FINISH LINE

We hurry
stumble
salivate
in the cooing of the clocks.
Then we beg for more time
in the famine
of our finish line.

ENIGMA OF EYES

It's a beautiful thing
the puzzle of our perception,
both sad with snowfall
and inflamed with ink.
We witness our worst
in the optimism of our optic nerves.

POINTING FINGERS

We hate the world for being around us.
The world hates us for being within.
Who will step out first?

STARS IN THE SUBJECT LINE

You wrote to me and put *Stars* in the subject line.
Hey. Want to be stars with me?
Darkness be damned, I thought.
Re: Okay. Let's be stars.

TOO MUCH

The ebony of emptiness on our earlobes
we listen to the chimes of the void,
chatter
from dust and debris,
we listen to the white noise
like a radio station
universe
reporting the weather
and the news
humming
on the vacancy of space
is always the same.

Still too much.
Still too much.

WINGS

Take a running start
and fly.

Isn't it what
plastic bags in the wind
dream of?

HOLINESS OF HOVERING STARS

A soul is
a shape of precipitation
and sea
    mine at least
carving out the crescent of my ribcage.
Such a dripping thing
claiming to be from the
holiness of hovering stars.

CHAPPED LIPS

People with chapped lips. That's what we are.
Dry and dusty. Sterile in our stardust.

USE BY

Souls go sour
waiting for
the expiration day of eternity.

CHIRP CHIRP

Slammed doors.
Useless wars.
Universe yelling *what*!?
And a mother bird feeding her chick a cigarette butt.

CIRCLE OF LIFE

It is this
burden of breathing,
this having to feel and fume,
to deflate and fill up
just to be
broken and
shared again and again
with stars that have temper.

Burn

And tell me again how
am I not supposed to grimace
with this mouthwash melancholy?

THINGS I DON'T SAY

I know
the unlit ivory of souls,
the seasick blue
of oceans.
I know
the sin of this
human-shaped shadow following me. I know.
I know!
I know!

AND STILL...

And just look at us
shaking   no! no! steady
so sure we can make it
and still
we get lost
in eternity's promises of pauses
while the dust of the once mighty
rattle in our respiration.

GRANOLA

Suppose
the holy water of this place
just drained out
a long time ago

you know
by accident
maybe

and the universe just never
fixed it
and now
we're the bowl
it eats cereal from
(might as well use it for something, right?)

or maybe granola
who knows

maybe we're the granola of this place
kind of crunchy and complicated
stuck in the teeth of stars.

GLITTER

Are we valued
by the pearls of our breaths?
The trinkets
we have for atoms?
Or the gems
subtle in the submarines of our souls?

PRETTY WAYS TO FALL

So powerful is my
cascading nature
that I write my will
on the back of every airline seat
and every balcony I see
I imagine all the possible suicides,
all the pretty ways to fall
and my sad outlines chalked below
for all the world to see.

VICE VERSA

The tar of this abyss
envies the beige of our being.

And vice versa, I believe.

HOW IT IS

Really.
It could be so different,
this
surface tension of a soul,
this
scattering of space,
this
cloudiness of our carcasses.
But this is how it is
and we shall keep scaling
the fingerprints of mountains
and name them after our every ache.

Born and raised in Helsinki, Finland, Heini Talip now resides in south Texas with her husband and cat. A writer and poet at heart since childhood, she has been published in two poetry anthologies. A proud vegan, she finds inspiration in her natural tendency to sadness, writing into words life's cloudiness that gives away to starry skies.

You can find her poetry on her Instagram:
@missfinnpoet

And on Amazon in:
Splintered Souls: An Anthology of Poems
Steady Hands: Ode to Our Fathers

www.ingramcontent.com/pod-product-compliance
Lightning Source LLC
LaVergne TN
LVHW041222080426
835508LV00011B/1037